BEGINNINGS

PLANTS

ORIGINS AND EVOLUTION

EVOLUTION OF THE UNIVERSE

4.5 billion years ago the oceans and first landmasses form.

9

1 million years after the Big Bang, hydrogen atoms form.

5

10-20 billion years ago, in less than a second, four things happen.

1. The Big Bang
2. Inflation
3. The beginning of the four forces
4. The first atomic nuclei form

1 billion years after the Big Bang, galaxies begin to form.

6

8   4.6 billion years ago the Earth's crust forms.

7   5 billion years ago the planet Earth forms.

11   2.5 billion years ago the atmosphere forms.

10   3 billion years ago bacteria appear— life begins.

BEGINNINGS

Plants

ORIGINS AND EVOLUTION

by
Alessandro Garassino

English Translation by Rocco Serini

Belitha Press

© Editoriale Jaca Book spa, Milan 1992

First published in the United Kingdom in 1994 by

Belitha Press Limited
31 Newington Green
London N16 9PU

English translation © 1994 by Steck-Vaughn Company.

Cataloguing in print data available from the British Library.

ISBN 1 85561 374 3

Photographic credits
Photographs DAVIDE CERIOLI, Nicorvo, Pavia: p. 37 (2). ALBERTO CONTRI, Milan: p. 8 (2), p. 16 (2), p. 33 (7, 8), p. 37 (4, 5). TONY CRADDOCK/GRAZIA NERI, Milan: p. 27 (4). RAFFAELE FATONE, Province of Borromeo, Milan: p. 9 (4, 5), p. 41 (5). ALESSANDRO GARASSINO, Milan: p. 40 (2). Editoriale Jaca Book, Milan (Carlo Scotti): p. 13 (4), p. 15 (3), p. 17 (5, 6), p. 21 (4), p. 25 (5, 7), p. 26 (1, 2, 3), p. 29 (5), p. 30 (1, 2, 3), p. 32 (2),p. 34 (1), p. 35 (3). JOHN G. MORRIS/W. EUGENE SMITH: p. 27 (5). GIOVANNI PINNA, Milan: p. 14 (1), p. 20 (2), p. 38 (1). MADALENA POCCIANTI, Scandicci, Florence: p. 17 (4). FABIO TERRANEO, Giussano, Milan: p. 39 (3). GIORGIO TERUZZI, Milan: p. 7 (3), p. 12 (3), p. 20 (1), p. 21 (3), p. 24 (1, 3), p. 34 (2).

Illustrations Editoriale Jaca Book, Milan (Cesare Dattena): p. 46-47; (Rosalba Moriggia and Maria Piatto): p. ii, p.iii, p. 8 (1), p. 10, p. 12 (stages), p. 17 (3), p. 28 (1, 2), p. 29 (3, 4), p. 31, p. 32 (1), p. 35 (4), p. 36 (1), p. 38 (2), p. 39 (4); (Lorenzo Orlandi): p. 12 (1); (Marco Rosso and Isabella Salmoirago): p. 19 (1), p. 22.
Illustrations p. 32 (3, 4, 5, 6), p. 33 (9, 10, 11), p. 40 (1, 3), p. 41 (4) are taken from *Flore Complète Illustrée en Couleurs de France, Suisse et Belgique* by Gaston Bonnor and Robert Douin, illustrated by Julie Poinsot, 13 vol., Librairie Générale de l'Enseignement Paris 1911-1935, republished in 2 vol. by Editions Belin, Paris 1990 (ediz. Ital. Editoriale Jaca Book, Milan 1990).
Illustration p. 12 (2), p. 13 (5), p. 14 (2), p. 16 (1), p. 18 (2, 3, 4, 5), p. 24 (2, 4, 6, 8), p. 31 (Archaeosperma) are from *Paleobotany and the Evolution of Plants* by Wilson N. Stewart, professor emeritus of Botany at University of Alberta, Edmonton, Canada, published by Cambridge University Press, Cambridge-New York-Melbourne 1983.

Graphics and Layout: The Graphics Department of Jaca Book.
Special thanks to the Museum of Natural History of Milan.

Printed and bound in the United States.

Contents

** The word billion is used
throughout this book to
mean one thousand million
or 1 000 000 000.*

The plant kingdom

When you walk in a garden, a wood, or even an overgrown building site, you see many different kinds of plants. Some are tall with thick, woody stems. Others grow along the ground with soft stems and colourful flowers. Some leaves are like needles, while others are thick and fleshy.

Species of plants develop over the generations. Major changes can lead to new members of a **species** evolving, or to a whole new species. The first living things were very simple. Over time they evolved into the enormous variety we find now. The chart shows that this process of evolution took many millions of years.

Learning from fossils

We can learn much about evolution from studying **fossils**, which are traces of animals and plants. Fossils tell us which species lived during each stage of Earth's development. We can see how species survived without changing, died out, or changed over time.

1 *This diagram shows the whole process of evolution in the plant kingdom. The first organisms evolved during the Precambrian Era, more than three billion years ago.*

These pictures show the great variety of stems, leaves, flowers and fruit which can be found in the plant kingdom: **2** *baobab;* **3** *ferns;* **4** *capers; and* **5** *elderberry.*

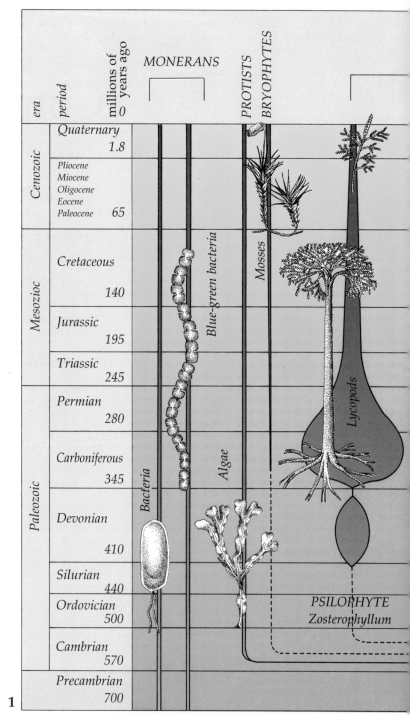

era	period	millions of years ago	MONERANS		PROTISTS	BRYOPHYTES	
Cenozoic	Quaternary	1.8					
	Pliocene Miocene Oligocene Eocene Paleocene	65					
Mesozoic	Cretaceous	140					
	Jurassic	195					
	Triassic	245					
Paleozoic	Permian	280					
	Carboniferous	345					
	Devonian	410					
	Silurian	440					
	Ordovician	500					
	Cambrian	570					
	Precambrian	700					

Blue-green bacteria · Mosses · Bacteria · Algae · Lycopods · PSILOPHYTE *Zosterophyllum*

1

2

3

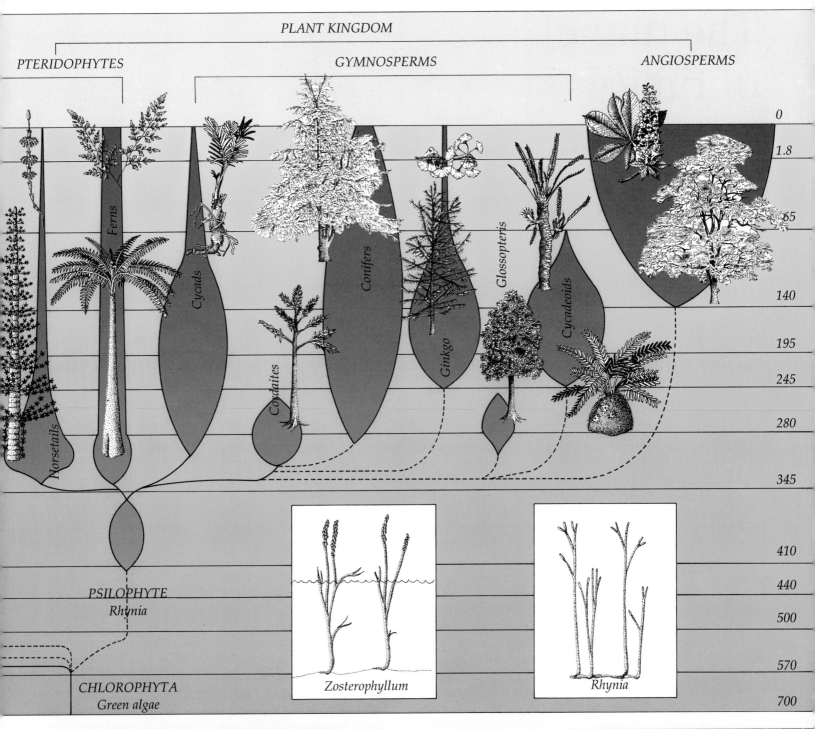

PLANT KINGDOM

PTERIDOPHYTES   GYMNOSPERMS   ANGIOSPERMS

0
1.8
65
140
195
245
280
345
410
440
500
570
700

Ferns

Horsetails

Cycads

Cordaites

Conifers

Ginkgo

Glossopteris

Cycadeoids

PSILOPHYTE
Rhynia

CHLOROPHYTA
Green algae

Zosterophyllum

Rhynia

4

5

9

The tunnel of time

Scientists have found that life on Earth began more than 3.5 billion years ago. Among the first living things were very simple **organisms** such as bacteria. These are tiny organisms which can only be seen through a microscope.

PTERIDOPHYTES
seedless vascular
plants
350 million years ago

PSILOPHYTES
primitive vascular plants
410 million
years ago

ALGAE
single-celled and
multicellular organisms
2500 million years ago

BACTERIA
BLUE-GREEN BACTERIA
monerans
3500 million years ago

Bacteria give off oxygen

Blue-green bacteria make their own food through **photosynthesis** (see page 39). They used carbon dioxide and water to do this, giving off **oxygen**. This build up of oxygen in our **atmosphere** over a long period of time enabled it to support a variety of plants and animals.

Green alga forms

Another group of organisms evolved from blue-green bacteria. These were green algae called chlorophyta. These algae are organized in a more complicated way than blue-green bacteria. Large algae with many **cells** evolved from chlorophyta and so did other types of plants that live on land.

Simple ferns evolve

The first plants were very small organisms made up of many cells, that lived in very damp areas. From these evolved simple ferns, the **psilophytes**. The whisk fern is one of the two surviving species of psilophytes. The two main groups of plants we see today evolved from early psilophytes. These are the **angiosperms**, or flowering plants, and the **gymnosperms**, or non-flowering plants.

10

GYMNOSPERMS
flowerless
seed plants
345 million years ago

ANGIOSPERMS
flowering seed plants
140 million years ago

The first forms of life

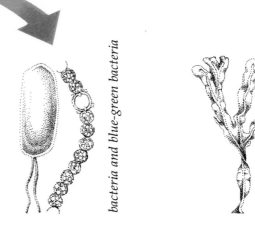

bacteria and blue-green bacteria

algae

The first living things on Earth were simple organisms. These organisms are called monerans. Bacteria are examples of monerans.

There is one type of bacteria which gets its energy from hot water and needs no oxygen. It is found only in sulphur-rich, hot pools. Few other organisms can live in such an environment. These bacteria use hydrogen sulphide (the compound which makes the smell of rotten eggs) to make their food. As hydrogen sulphide is a gas given off by volcanoes it was probably very common in the Earth's early atmosphere.

All sorts of bacteria

There are other bacteria which do not live in water. Some need oxygen. Others can live without it. But all types of bacteria are very simple, microscopic organisms. Their structure is very simple. Bacteria may be round, rod-shaped, or spiral-shaped. Some types of bacteria may be linked together in clumps or in long chains.

Blue-green bacteria

At some point, blue-green bacteria evolved. Unlike other types of bacteria, they could make food by photosynthesis. The blue-green bacteria gave off so much oxygen that they changed the atmosphere. Blue-green bacteria are found today in fresh and salt water, often living in large masses.

Widespread fossils

Fossils of bacteria have been found in Canada, South Africa and Australia. Studies on fossils such as Ainimikiea, Archaeonema and Palaeolyngbya, show that they are very similar to the bacteria and blue-green bacteria of today.

1

2 3

psilophytes

pteridophytes

gymnosperms

angiosperms

4

Archaeonema

Palaeolyngbya

Ainimikiea

5

1 *An artist's impression of bacteria in the first seas.*

2 *This fossil is similar to the bacteria which are common today. It is Gunflintia, found in Gunflint Formation, Canada.*

3 *These thick mats of bacteria, blue-green bacteria and sand in Shark Bay, Australia, are similar to those that lived billions of years ago. They are called stromatolites. The mats build up as sand sticks to a substance given off by the organisms. When the sand covers the bacteria, they move up through it and again attract more sand. In this way they form new layers.*

4 *The section of fossil on the left is Collenia nudosa, a stromatolite which was found in Minnesota. A different type of stromatolite from Cochabamba, Bolivia, is shown on the right. Both fossils belong to the Precambrian Era and are about two billion years old.*

5 *These pairs of blue-green bacteria show that the species have changed very little over time. Blue-green bacteria found today (on the left side of each pair) are similar to their fossil ancestors (shown on the right).*

Algae

Algae are plants which are found near water. At one time scientists classified the blue-green bacteria as algae, thinking of them as simple plants. This was because the blue-green bacteria make their own food through photosynthesis, have a cell wall and **chlorophyll** – the **pigment** plants need for photosynthesis. Unlike algae, the blue-green bacteria do not have a nucleus or other structures in their cells. This simple structure makes the organisms more like monerans than algae. Scientists have generally reclassified them as monerans.

Some scientists are not sure that algae should be classified as plants. Some think that algae belong in the group called protists. Protists are micro-organisms which have only one cell, with a nucleus and other structures.

Early algae

The first algae lived about 2.5 billion years ago. By then there was enough oxygen in the water to support their growth. Scientists think that all modern plants evolved from the chlorophyta, or green algae. The first green algae were probably tiny single-celled organisms.

As algae evolved they became able to **reproduce** sexually.

Algae today

Simpler algae evolved into the many kinds of algae living today. These include the giant kelps and other brown algae, as well as the red algae which include most types of seaweeds. Other adaptations developed as new species of plants evolved which could live on land.

There are present-day green algae which measure more than six metres long but many modern species consist of single cells. They live in fresh or salt water.

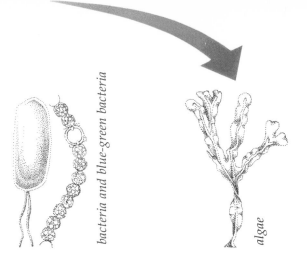

bacteria and blue-green bacteria

algae

1

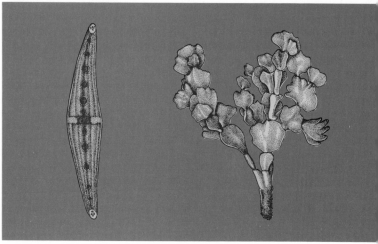

2

psilophytes

pteridophytes

gymnosperms

angiosperms

3

1 *Fucus vesiculosus is a species of brown alga found living off the coasts of the United States and other temperate waters.*
2 *Algae include Closterium, Halimeda, Chara, and Acetabularia.*
3 *Fossils of Diplopora annulata were found in a rock from Italy. They probably date from the Triassic Period about 200 million years ago.*

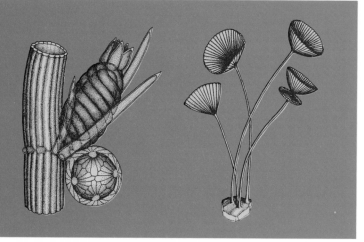

First plants on land

Billions of years ago the earliest forms of life began in water. Water contained the nutrients which these organisms needed. Living in water also helped the process of reproduction.

Plants adapt to land

More than 400 million years ago living things spread from the water and onto land. On the land there are carbon dioxide and sunshine which the plants needed for photosynthesis. To survive on land plants needed a way to move the nutrients from the soil up the stem of the plant to the leaves. For this they developed **vascular tissues**, which were made up of hollow cells. They also needed to be able to reproduce away from water.

Fossils of early plants

These can be found in many parts of the world, including the United States, Canada and England. Some date from the **Silurian Period** about 420 million years ago and the **Devonian Period**, about 395 million years ago.

One of the earliest fossil plants was Cooksonia, which was about six centimetres tall. It vanished without leaving any descendants. Modern plants probably evolved from two similar types of psilophytes that lived during the Devonian Period. Zosterophyllum was about 20 centimetres tall, with thin stems and branches. Plants such as club **mosses**, which are called **lycopods**, evolved from this. Rhynia, a reedlike plant, is about 15 centimetres tall. Scientists believe that most of the plants we know today evolved from Rhynia.

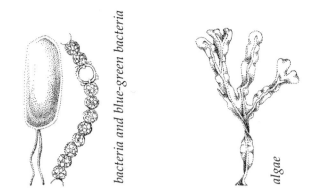

bacteria and blue-green bacteria

algae

1 *An artist's impression of what a swamp in the Devonian Period, about 400 million years ago, may have looked like. Many of the plants had developed branched stems but not leaves. Plants shown, from left to right, are Zosterophyllum rehenanum, Asteroxylon mackiei and Rhynia major.*

2 *Cooksonia calendonica is one of the oldest fossil plants. It lived about 420 million years ago. The reproductive organ, which contained spores, is shown on the left.*

3, 4 *and 5 show plants of the Devonian Period. From left to right they are Zosterophyllum rehenanum, Asteroxylon mackiei and Psilophyton dawsonii.*

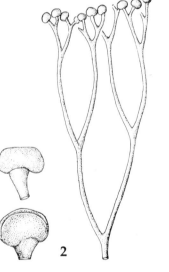

3   4   5

psilophytes

pteridophytes

gymnosperms

angiosperms

1

Bryophytes and vascular plants

Not long after plants spread onto land, they evolved into two separate groups – the **bryophytes** and the vascular plants.

Small plants in moist places

Bryophytes are relatively small, simple plants that have not developed special **tissues** to carry nutrients to the leaves. Water moves slowly through this type of plant, from one cell to the next. Because of this, a bryophyte cannot grow very large. Most are found in very moist areas.

Bryophyte fossils have been found as early as the Devonian Period. Some are very similar to bryophytes living today. Modern bryophytes include the mosses, liverworts and hornworts.

Tall plants far from water

The other major group of land plants were the vascular plants. These have developed tissues which carry materials throughout the plant. The tissues form tubes that carry water and food, rather like the tubes which carry your blood around your body. Vascular tissue allows these plants to grow into tall trees and to live far from water.

Vascular plants have roots, leaves and stems. The roots grow down into the soil, anchoring the plant and taking in water and nutrients. Leaves are used for photosynthesis. Stems support the plants, grow thick with vascular tissue and hold leaves up to the sunlight.

Trees of stone

Fossils of the earliest vascular plants are about 400 million years old. Some of the most impressive fossils of ancient vascular plants can be found in petrified forests. Here minerals have gradually replaced the plant tissue, forming trees of stone.

2 *Present-day mosses live close to the ground and are similar in structure to ancient forms.*

1 *The moss Sporogonites exuberans lived during the Devonian Period, about 400 million years ago. The reproductive organs were on top of thin stems.*

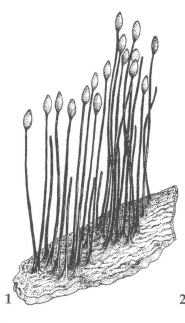

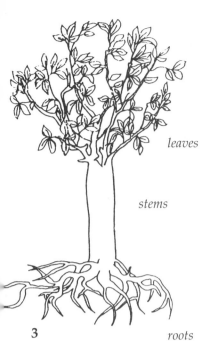

leaves

stems

3

roots

4

5

3 Vascular plants have evolved roots, stems and leaves.

4 These petrified logs are in Petrified Forest National Park, Arizona.

5 This section of a petrified log shows how water filled with minerals seeped in as the tree rotted away. The log is now made up largely of quartz. The red areas are formed by iron oxides.

6 This fossilized trunk shows details of the tree from which it was formed.

6

Carboniferous forests

The **Carboniferous Period** lasted from about 345 to 280 million years ago. At that time the Earth's **climate** was generally warm and moist. Even North America and Europe had tropical climates.

Plants did very well in this environment. Some vascular plants reproduced through spreading **spores** (see page 31). These are called **pteridophytes**. Some of them grew very tall. This meant they could reach sunlight and could spread their spores over a large area. More new plants could grow.

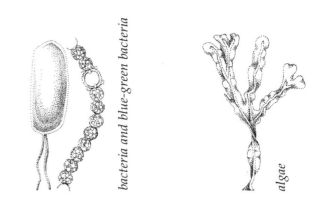

bacteria and blue-green bacteria

algae

Trees of the forests

Great swamp forests covered much of the land. These were filled with giant tree ferns, lycopod trees and horsetails. Although club mosses found today are very small, the closely-related, giant lycopod trees were the biggest in the Carboniferous forests. The most common lycopod was the Lepidodendron, which grew up to 40 metres tall. Sigillaria, another lycopod, grew up to 20 metres. These giant lycopods are now **extinct**.

Tree-sized horsetails were also common in the swamp forests. One type, Calamites, grew up to 10 metres tall. Horsetails can still be found today but they are all small plants. The tall horsetail species of the Carboniferous Period are now extinct.

Tree ferns are the only giant survivors of the pteridophytes. They are usually found in tropical forests but smaller ferns can be found in most parts of the world. During the Carboniferous Period, the species Psaronius grew to about three metres tall.

Gymnosperms could also be found in the Carboniferous swamp forests. One gymnosperm, Cordaitales, grew to 40 metres tall. It is now extinct.

1

2

*These four photos show fossils of giant horsetails of the Carboniferous Period: **1** foliage of Annularia; **2** and **3** fragments of the trunks of Calamites; **4** foliage of Annularia, found in Illinois, United States.*

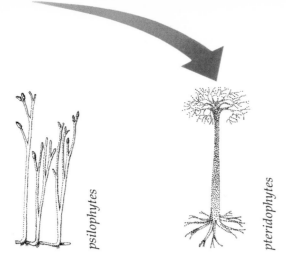

psilophytes

pteridophytes

gymnosperms

angiosperms

On pages 22 and 23 is an artist's impression of a Carboniferous forest 34.5 million years ago. You can see the giant lycopods, Lepidodendron and Sigillaria; the giant horsetail, Calamites; the tree fern, Psaronius; and the gymnosperm, Cordaitales. The first reptiles were appearing.

3

4

Fossils of the Carboniferous Period

1

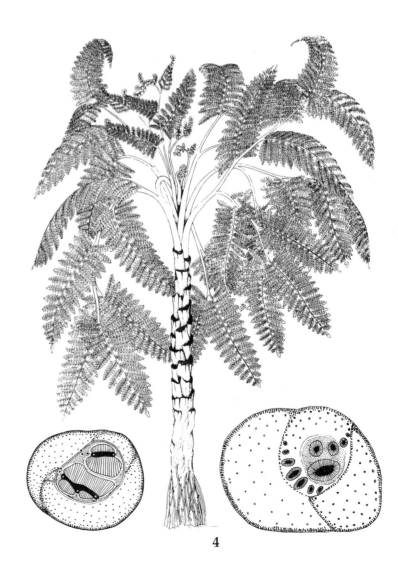

2

1 This fragment of a fossil trunk of Cordaites was found in Germany. It dates from the Carboniferous Period.
2 Cordaites had long leaves and shoots extending from the branches.
3 This fossil of a fern-like fossil was found in Illinois, United States.
4 Medullosa was a fern-like tree which had seeds and was one of the earliest gymnosperms. At the bottom you can see cross-sections of a branch. The one on the left shows two tubes of vascular tissue. That on the right shows several tubes.

3

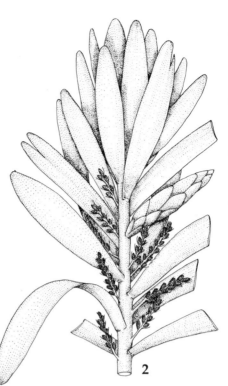

4

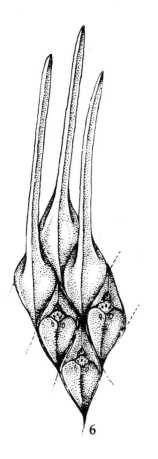

6

The giant lycopods of the
Carboniferous Period: **5** section of
Lepidodendron showing leaves and
leaf scars; **6** fossils of Lepidodendron
showing diamond-shaped leaf scars;
7 leaf scars of Sigillaria; **8** fragments
of a fossil trunk of Sigillaria showing
six-sided leaf scars.

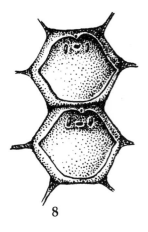

8

5

7

Coal deposits

The great forests of 300 million years ago that developed, grew, and died out hundreds of millions of years ago are very important to us today. They are the source of fossil fuels – coal, petroleum and natural gas.

Coal is formed

The plants which lived in the swamp forests were tall but they had shallow roots. Strong winds easily knocked them over. Often the trees would totally sink into the **marshy** ground before they had completely rotted away. Sediments would cover them. The partially decayed trees turned into a spongy substance called **peat**. Later sedimentary rock covered and pressed down on the peat. If there were the proper conditions, such as the right temperature, the peat gradually turned into coal.

Different types of coal

The first type of coal to form is called **lignite**. This is a fairly soft coal. After a longer period of time, lignite can change into **bituminous coal**. Later still it can change into **anthracite** which is the oldest, hardest and most valuable coal.

1

3

2

4

5

1 *Anthracite coal is hard and black. It formed during the Paleozoic Era.*
2 *Bituminous coal is softer than anthracite and formed during the Paleozoic, Mesozoic and Cenozoic eras.*
3 *Peat formed during the Cenozoic Era.*
4 *This strip mine covers an area of about five square kilometres and yields up to 110 000 cubic metres of coal per day. The excavator is so large that it had to be built on the site and took two years to build.*
5 *Underground mines such as this one in South Wales do not destroy the countryside. However, they are dangerous places to work. Miners are sometimes trapped in the mines, and they may die of lung disease caused by coal dust.*

Plants in the Permian Period

The **Permian Period** came after the Carboniferous Period. It was a time of great change lasting from about 280 to 245 million years ago. At the start of the period, all the landmasses on Earth had moved together to form one huge continent called Pangaea. As the continents moved, their climates changed. Land that had once been covered by tropical forests became drier and colder. The pteridophytes, the giant horsetails, tree ferns and lycopods that had been so important in the forests of the Carboniferous Period, began to die out.

Seed plants in the north

Seed plants came to dominate the northern part of Pangaea. They had begun to appear during the Carboniferous Period. They reproduced by making seeds (see page 32). As the climate became drier seed plants reproduced more successfully than the pteridophytes which spread by their spores.

Forests in the south

The climate was colder in the southern part of the continent. Here vast forests grew up. Dominating these forests was a non-flowering plant called Glossopteris, which is now extinct. This tree grew to a height of about six metres. It had long, lance-shaped leaves. Fossils of these leaves have been found in places as far apart as South America and Australia, South Africa and Antarctica. The fact that these fossils have been found in such widely separated areas is evidence for the idea that the continents were at one time joined together.

1 The continents were widely spaced around the Earth about 345 million years ago.
2 The continents came together and formed one large continent about 280 million years ago. We call this continent Pangaea. It had two main parts – Laurasia in the north and Gondwana in the south.

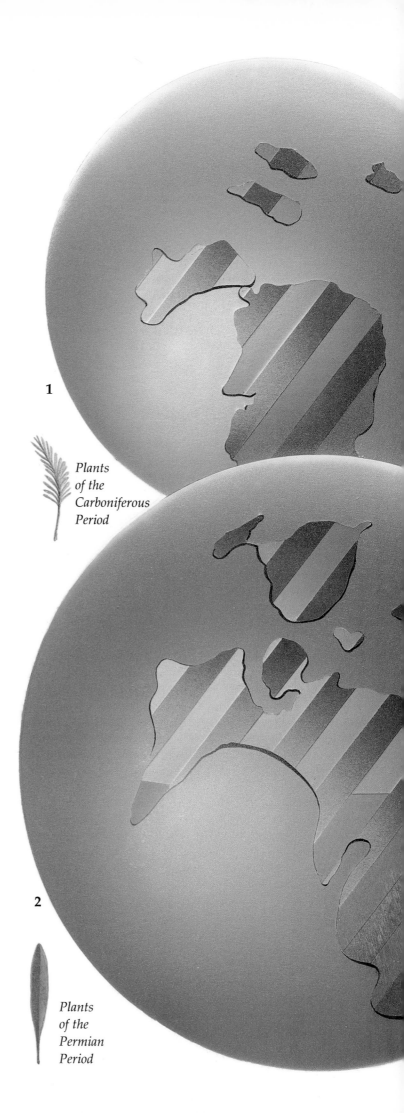

1

Plants of the Carboniferous Period

2

Plants of the Permian Period

3 The Glossopteris dominated the forests of Gondwana.
4 The leaf of the Glossopteris was shaped like a lance and had parallel veins.
5 These fossils from Australia show the leaves of Glossopteris.

Gymnosperms – non-flowering plants

When plants first began to grow on land, they still lived near the sea or in marshy areas.

Plants evolved with a waterproof coating to prevent drying out. Once they were waterproofed, plants needed a way to absorb and transport water. To meet these needs, plants evolved with roots which could absorb water, and vascular tissue to carry the water to all parts. There was still one remaining challenge. How could the plants form new plants without being in water?

Beginning of seed plants

Seed plants met this challenge. Seeds allowed plants to reproduce sexually without a constant supply of water. You will learn more about seeds on pages 32 and 33. The first type of seed plants were gymnosperm, or non-flowering plants.

Gymnosperm fossils

Fossils of an early type of gymnosperm, Archaeosperma, have been found in Scotland and probably date from the end of the Devonian Period, about 345 million years ago. Many more gymnosperm fossils have been found from the Carboniferous Period.

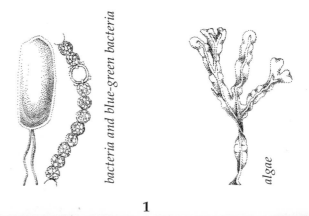

bacteria and blue-green bacteria

algae

1

2

1 *The two parts of this fossil show a pine cone from the Miocene Era, about 26 million years ago.*

2 *and* 3 *Fossil imprints of the branches of a monkey-puzzle tree from about 136 million years ago.*

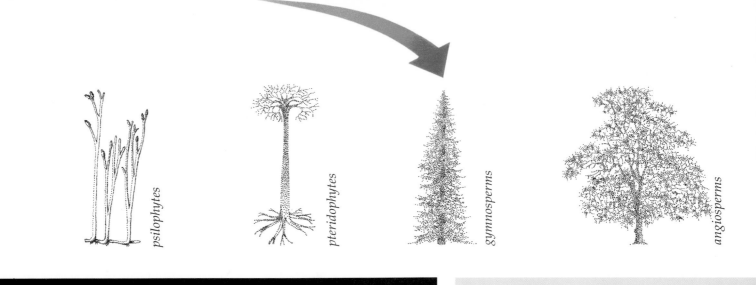

psilophytes

pteridophytes

gymnosperms

angiosperms

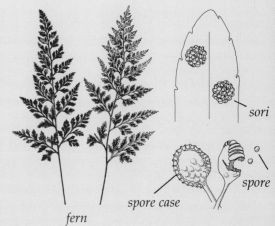

sori

spore

spore case

fern

Ferns reproduce by means of spores.
They develop inside spore cases called sori.
When a spore is released it develops into a
tiny plant. This plant produces sperm and
eggs but these need water in order to unite
and grow into a mature fern plant.
The egg and sperm of a seed plant unite on
the parent plant. Here there is water and
protection. The seeds are protected within the
stem of this gymnosperm, *Archaeosperma*.

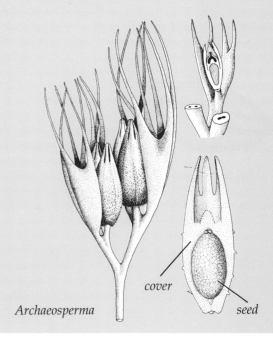

cover

seed

Archaeosperma

Seeds

Some vascular plants used spores for reproduction. Spores can only form a new plant if they have a constant supply of water. Otherwise they easily dry out. If there is not enough rainfall, or any other water, this type of plant cannot reproduce.

Sexual reproduction

Making seeds was a giant step in the evolution of plants. The female sex cell stayed attached to the plant. The male sex cell united with it. The **embryo** of a new plant could develop, protected by the parent plant. A hard, waterproof covering surrounded the embryo and its food supply. When ready, this could be shed from the plant. This little package was the seed.

The seed would sprout when conditions were right. If the ground was hard and dry, or if it was too cold, nothing would happen. The seed would only sprout and grow when there was enough rain and warmth. This makes seed plants more adaptable than non-seed plants to changing climate. Thus the first seed plants, gymnosperms, were at an advantage when the climate changed during the Permian Period.

wing

embryo

endosperm

1 *The wing attached to this seed is easily lifted by the wind. It may land far from the parent plant. The embryo will develop into a new plant when the conditions are right. While the embryo is growing nutrients are supplied by the endosperm.*

2 *Pine cone fossils from the Jurassic Period, about 170 million years ago.*

3 *Larix europaea* pine cones.
4 *Abies pectinata* pine cone.
5 *Pinus pinea* pine cone.
6 *Pinus maritima* pine cone.
7 Larch.
8 Fir trees.
9 *Pinus halepensis*.
10 *Abies pectinata*.
11 *Pinus cembra*.

7

8

9

10

11

Living fossils

Charles Darwin first set out the theory of evolution in the nineteenth century. He described the ginkgo tree as a 'living fossil' because it has survived, almost unchanged, for millions of years. Many other living fossils have been found since. Some are plants, some are animals. All have survived for hundreds of millions of years.

Ginkgo biloba

This plant was found in temple gardens in East Asia. It is now commonly planted in the United States and elsewhere. The ginkgo is a gymnosperm but it is unusual in that it is not an evergreen. In autumn fan-shaped leaves turn bright yellow and drop from the tree.

The cycad

Another type of gymnosperm that has survived with little change is the cycad. The *Cycas revoluta*, sometimes called the false palm, can be found in parks and gardens in the United States and Europe.

Giant sequoia

One other gymnosperm living fossil is the giant **sequoia** tree. Some giant sequoias may be the oldest living things on Earth. They are also some of the largest. The General Sherman Tree in California is more than 2000 years old. It measures 82.5 metres tall and over 30 metres around its base. Giant sequoias grow only in the Sierra Nevada Mountains of California.

1 *The fan-shaped leaves of the Ginkgo biloba.*
2 *Cycas revoluta is a cycad not a palm.*
3 *This rock contains a ginkgo fossil. It was found in the United States and is thought to be about 60 million years old.*
4 *The living fossils of today with their fossil ancestors. The three plants on the left are ferns. The four on the right are gymnosperms.*

3

Quaternary		*Angiopteris*	*Dipteris*	*Matonia*	*Ginkgo biloba*	*Cycas*	*Araucaria*	*Sequoia*
Tertiary								
Cretaceous								
Jurassic		*Clathropteris*	*Matonidium*	*Ginkgoidium*	*Cycadites*	*Araucaria*	*Sequoia*
Triassic								
Permian	*Danaeopsis*							

4

Angiosperms – flowering plants

Living things have to adapt as the world changes. Those that are the best adapted are the most successful. In the beginning, the simplest organisms, bacteria, were the most successful. Much later came the age of the dinosaur. Today could be called the age of the angiosperms. Angiosperms, or flowering plants, are everywhere. They are the roses in your garden, the grass on your lawn, the oak which gives you shade, the wheat in the fields, and even the broccoli on your plate.

Colours and scents

Some of the plants which are called angiosperms may only have tiny flowers. You may not notice the flowers of an oak tree or a grass plant. They are not large or brightly coloured. Coloured flowers evolved in some species to improve chances of **pollination**, an essential part of the reproduction process. The colourful petals and scent of the flower attract

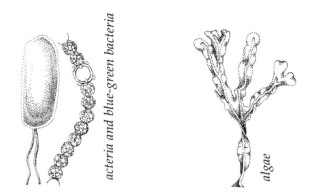

bacteria and blue-green bacteria

algae

insects and other animals. While gathering nectar, a bee will be dusted with the **pollen** in a flower. Moving to the next flower, some of the pollen comes off the bee, thus spreading pollen from one flower to the next.

Another important feature of angiosperms is that their seeds develop inside fruits.

Fossils of angiosperms

Flowering plants first evolved at the beginning of the **Cretaceous Period**, about 140 million years ago. Fossils of early angiosperms have been found in North and South America as well as in Europe and Africa.

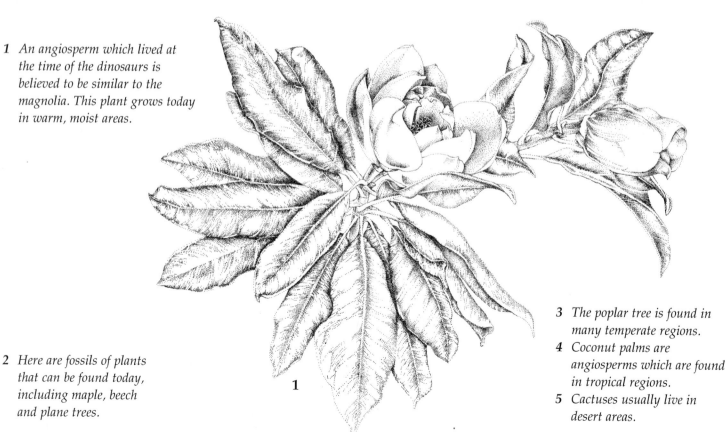

1 *An angiosperm which lived at the time of the dinosaurs is believed to be similar to the magnolia. This plant grows today in warm, moist areas.*

2 *Here are fossils of plants that can be found today, including maple, beech and plane trees.*

3 *The poplar tree is found in many temperate regions.*

4 *Coconut palms are angiosperms which are found in tropical regions.*

5 *Cactuses usually live in desert areas.*

psilophytes

pteridophytes

gymnosperms

angiosperms

3

2

4

5

Flowers

Flowers enable flowering plants to reproduce. Flowers have male and female parts. The anthers which are at the tip of the **stamens**, produce and store pollen. The pollen contains male sex cells. It is moved, usually by wind or by insects, to the **stigma** of a flower, at the tip of the **pistil**. From there, a male sex cell moves down the pistil to a female sex cell. This is inside the **ovary** at the base of the pistil. The two sex cells unite and form an embryo, a very early stage of a new plant. The embryo, plus stored food, is surrounded by a tough outer coat to make a seed.

1

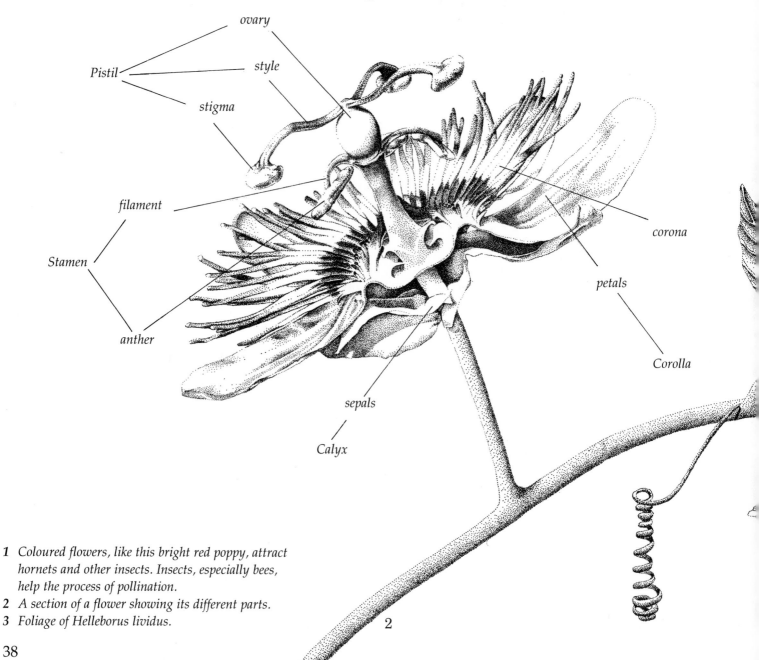

ovary

Pistil — style

stigma

filament

Stamen

anther

corona

petals

Corolla

sepals

Calyx

2

1 *Coloured flowers, like this bright red poppy, attract hornets and other insects. Insects, especially bees, help the process of pollination.*
2 *A section of a flower showing its different parts.*
3 *Foliage of Helleborus lividus.*

38

and Leaves

Leaves have two main functions.

Releasing water

Leaves release water through tiny pores in their surface. This process is called **transpiration**. Water is pulled up through the plant's vascular tissue, just as it is sucked through a straw.

Absorbing energy

Photosynthesis is a complex process in which sugar is formed from carbon dioxide and water. Chlorophyll is the pigment which makes plants green. This absorbs energy from sunlight. Oxygen is given off as a waste product.

3

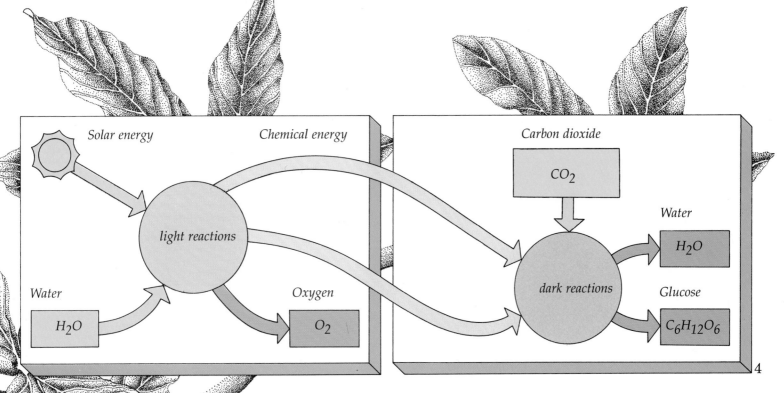

Solar energy   Chemical energy   Carbon dioxide

CO_2

light reactions

Water

H_2O Oxygen O_2

Water

H_2O

dark reactions   Glucose

$C_6H_{12}O_6$

4

4 *This diagram shows the two-step process of photosynthesis. In the first step, chlorophyll takes in energy from sunlight and changes it to chemical energy stored by hydrogen. In the second step, the plant uses this chemical energy to change carbon dioxide into glucose, which is a form of sugar. In photosynthesis, the plant uses carbon dioxide and gives out oxygen.*

Fruit

After seeds have formed in the ovaries of a flower, the ovaries become larger and grow into fruits. The fruit protects the seeds. It may also help scatter the seeds. Some fruits break open when they ripen, and wind carries the seeds away. Other types of fruit are eaten by animals. After the fruit is eaten, the seeds are usually passed out of the body of the animal. They may fall into the soil far away from the parent plant and grow into new plants.

All kinds of fruit

Fruits can be classified into several types. Fleshy fruits are some of the most common, such as peaches, cherries or plums. **Aggregate** fruits, such as strawberries or blackberries, appear to be a single fruit but are actually made up of many tiny fruits. Some other foods that we may not think of as fruits, such as peas, wheat and poppies, are classified as dry fruits.

1 Blackberries are an aggregate fruit.
2 Breadfruit grows on tall trees in islands in the Pacific.
3 An apricot is an example of a fleshy fruit.
4 Grains are classified as dry fruits.
5 These chilli peppers are the fruit of chilli plants.

2

3

40

4   5

Glossary

aggregate: a collection; in fruit, a collection of smaller fruits joined together.

angiosperm: a flowering seed plant.

anthracite: the oldest and hardest type of coal.

atmosphere: the gases that surround the Earth.

baobab: an African tree with a thick trunk and edible fruit (see page 8).

bituminous coal: a form of coal harder and older than lignite, but softer and younger than anthracite.

bryophytes: simple plants, such as mosses, that lack vascular tissue.

calyx: the outer leaflike parts of a flower that surround the petals (see page 38).

caper: the edible flower bud of a low shrub (see page 8).

Carboniferous Period: a period of the Paleozoic Era in the history of the Earth, when many coal beds formed (see page 8).

cell: the basic unit of all living things.

chlorophyll: the green pigment, or colouring, contained in plants. Chlorophyll traps light and converts it into a form of energy that plants can use to make food.

climate: the typical weather in an area.

corolla: the ring of petals, usually coloured, that make up a flower (see page 38).

Cretaceous Period: the third period of the Mesozoic Era in the history of the Earth (see page 8).

Devonian Period: a period in the Paleozoic Era in the history of the Earth (see page 8).

embryo: the earliest stage in the development of an organism.

endosperm: tissue inside a seed, which stores food (see page 32).

era: a unit of time; in the history of the Earth, an era is subdivided into periods (see page 8).

extinct: a species that has died out is extinct.

fossil: the preserved remains or trace of organisms that lived in the past.

gymnosperm: a plant whose seeds are not enclosed in a fruit.

lignite: a soft brownish-black coal.

lycopods: vascular plants that thrived as large trees during the Carboniferous Period. Club mosses are living examples of lycopods.

magnolia: a flowering shrub or tree with large, waxlike, fragrant flowers (see page 36).

marsh: an area of wetland filled with plants.

monkey-puzzle: a Chilean pine tree (see page 30).

moss: a small, simple nonvascular plant that often grows in tufts or clusters on decaying wood, the ground, or rocks.

organism: a living thing, either animal or plant.

ovary: in plants, a structure in which the female sex cells as well as the seeds develop.

oxygen: an odourless and colourless gas found in air and water and needed by most living things.

peat: a partly decomposed, partially carbonized plant material.

Permian Period: the last period of the Paleozoic Era in the history of the Earth (see page 8).

photosynthesis: a process in which plants produce food using water, carbon dioxide and sunlight.

pigment: organic colouring matter that gives animals and plants their colour.

pistil: the female part of a flower.

pollen: fine grains in seed plants that contain sperm.

pollination: the process in which pollen is carried from the male to the female parts of a plant.

psilophytes: simple plants from which most modern plants are thought to have evolved.

pteridophytes: vascular plants that reproduce by means of spores.

reproduction: the process by which living things produce their young.

sepal: one of the individual leaves of the calyx of a flower (see page 38).

sequoia: a gigantic evergreen tree of the western United States, also called a giant redwood.

Silurian Period: a period of the Paleozoic Era (see page 8).

sori: the tiny caplike structures made up of clusters of sporangia. Sori are found on the bottom of fern leaves (see page 29).

species: the smallest classification group of groups of organisms, for example horse chestnuts (*Aesculus hippocastanum*) and sweet chestnuts (*Castanea sativa*) are members of different species.

spore: structures given off by non-seed vascular plants which develop into a small plant where sexual reproduction takes place.

stamen: a male part of the flower.

stigma: the tip of the pistil.

stromatolites: an abundant fossil form of bacteria and blue-green bacteria (see page 38).

style: the part of the pistil that connects the stigma and ovary (see page 38).

tissue: a group of cells that have the same origin and the same functions in an organism.

transpiration: a process in which plants give off water into the atmosphere.

vascular tissue: specialized tissue that moves materials, especially water, through a plant.

Index

Numbers in **bold** refer to illustrations.

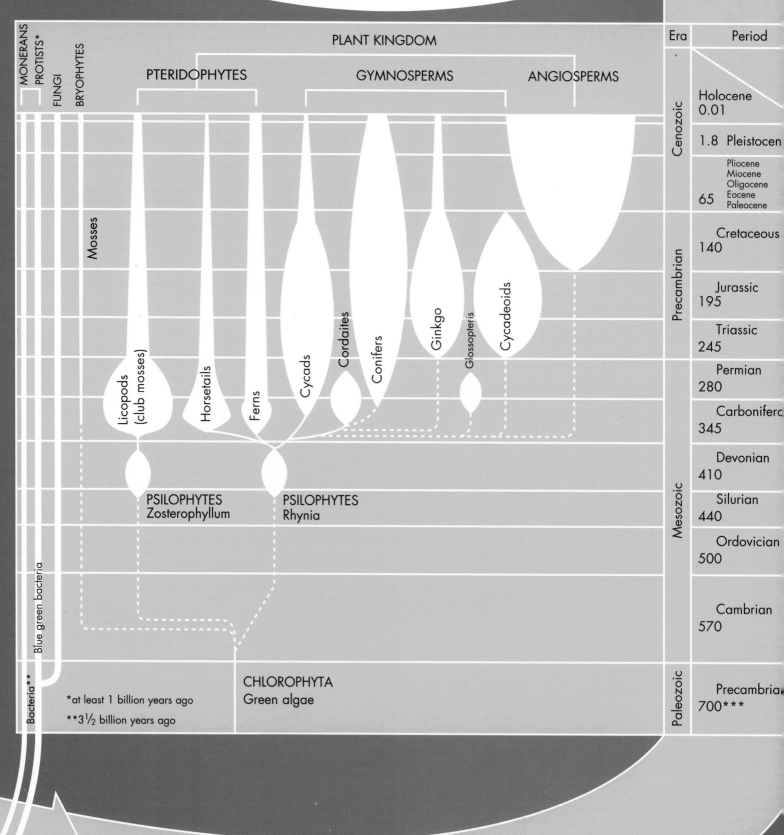

EVOLUTION OF THE MONERAN, PROTIST, PLANT, AND FUNGI KINGDOMS

MONERANS

PROTISTS*

FUNGI

BRYOPHYTES

PLANT KINGDOM

PTERIDOPHYTES

GYMNOSPERMS

ANGIOSPERMS

Mosses

Licopods (club mosses)

Horsetails

Ferns

Cycads

Cordaites

Conifers

Ginkgo

Glossopteris

Cycadeoids

PSILOPHYTES
Zosterophyllum

PSILOPHYTES
Rhynia

Blue green bacteria

Bacteria**

CHLOROPHYTA
Green algae

*at least 1 billion years ago

**3 1/2 billion years ago

Era	Period
Cenozoic	Holocene 0.01
	1.8 Pleistocen
	Pliocene / Miocene / Oligocene / Eocene / Paleocene 65
Precambrian	Cretaceous 140
	Jurassic 195
	Triassic 245
Mesozoic	Permian 280
	Carbonifero 345
	Devonian 410
	Silurian 440
	Ordovician 500
	Cambrian 570
Paleozoic	Precambria 700***

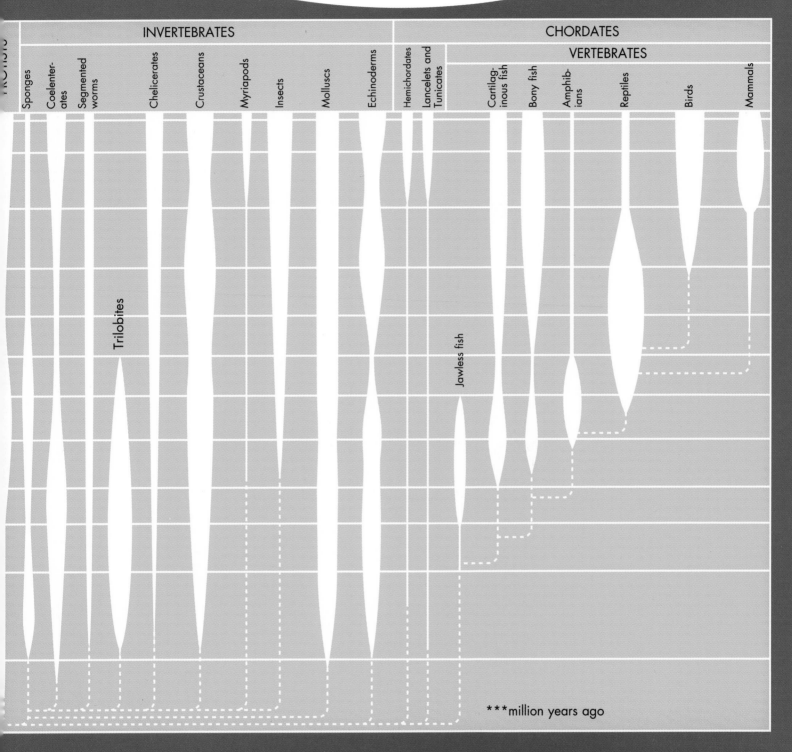

EVOLUTION OF THE PROTIST AND ANIMAL KINGDOMS

INVERTEBRATES

CHORDATES

VERTEBRATES

PROTISTS

Sponges

Coelenter-ates

Segmented worms

Chelicerates

Crustaceans

Myriapods

Insects

Molluscs

Echinoderms

Hemichordates

Lancelets and Tunicates

Cartilag-inous fish

Bony fish

Amphib-ians

Reptiles

Birds

Mammals

Trilobites

Jawless fish

***million years ago